THE MASTERPIECES OF

THE
HERMITAGE

STATE HALLS AND
PRIVATE ROOMS

WESTERN EUROPEAN
PAINTING AND SCULPTURE
FROM THE 15TH THROUGH
THE 20TH CENTURIES

IMPRESSIONISM AND
POST-IMPRESSIONISM

RUSSIAN AND EUROPEAN
DECORATIVE AND
APPLIED ART

ORIENTAL AND
NEAR-EASTERN ART

THE GOLDEN
DRAWING-ROOM

SLAVIA

BB
BONECHI

General Editor *Dr. Mikhail Piotrovsky*

Conception by *Olga Fedosseyenko*
Introduced by *Liudmila Torshina*
Annotations by *Olga Fedosseyenko, Anna Barkhatova*
Translated from the Russian by *Alexandra George,
Irina Stukalina*
Photographs by *Vladimir Terebenin, Leonard Kheifets*

Edited by *Anna Barkhatova, Olga Fedosseyenko*
Editor of the English text *Irina Stukalina*
Design and computer-aided makeup by *Yelena Polenova*
Design of the cover by *Rosanna Malagrino*

© The State Hermitage, St. Petersburg, 2004
© Slavia, St. Petersburg, 2004
© Casa Editrice Bonechi, Florence, 2004
ISBN 5-88654-092-X

The Hermitage is a celebrated museum, the pride of Russia and her northern capital, St. Petersburg. The Hermitage houses more than three and a half million monuments of art and culture. These include paintings, sculptures, drawings and engravings, the richest collection of works of the applied arts and more than one million coins and medals and archaeological and cultural artefacts. In the Hermitage the entire history of culture and art of the peoples of Europe and the East from the most ancient times until the twentieth century appears before the visitor.

The Hermitage occupies five buildings in the centre of St. Petersburg being one of the most beautiful architectural ensembles. It includes the Winter Palace, the former residence of the Russian emperors, the Hermitage Theatre and also the museum buildings proper: the Small, Old and New Hermitages.

The exhibition dedicated to the early eighteenth-century history of Russian culture is displayed in the Menshikov Palace on Vasilyevsky Island.

The museum was initiated in 1764 when Empress Catherine II owned the Berlin merchant Johann Ernest Gotzkowski's collection of 225 paintings. She made it her goal to establish her own palace gallery which would possess collections no less famous than those of European monarchs. On her instruction, through the intermediaries of the best art connoisseurs of the time, both entire collections, as well as individual works of art, were purchased at European auctions; and commissions were made from prominent artists. The Empress gave herself up with passion to the collection of gemstones. By her own admission she suffered from the "gemstone sickness". Towards the close of Catherine II's reign the Hermitage collection numbered 3,000 paintings, almost 7,000 drawings and more than 70,000 engravings, as well as 10,000 carved stones and 38,000 books. Already at that time the Hermitage was considered to possess one of the richest palatial collections in Europe. In the subsequent era following Catherine the Great's reign, additions to the Hermitage became more and more systematized: the museum acquired monuments of art which were needed to provide a comprehensive reflection of the history of art.

Thus in the 1830–1860s antique relics were actively purchased in Europe; the largest acquisition of the Empress at that time was the Marquis of Campana's famous collection. In the 1830s archaeological research began in southern Russia and the Hermitage was enriched with the most valuable works of ancient Greek and Scythian art.

From a private palatial museum such as it was under Catherine II, the Hermitage by the mid-nineteenth century had already been transformed into the most outstanding European museum of world art.

The immense palace of the Russian emperors, built in the eighteenth-century Baroque style, is a majestic and elegant edifice. Its southern façade with wide patterned cast-iron gates, with mighty columns spanning two stories and with sculptures over the cornice, faces Dvortsovaya (Palace) Square. The northern façade with its high porch stretched along the Neva, with its rhythm of snow-white columns echoing the coursing of the river's waves, as it were.

The western and eastern façades with their rezalites are turned towards the city: the eastern part is hidden behind

The State Hermitage. Panoramic view from the Neva

The Winter Palace in St. Petersburg is one of the most wonderful creations of Francesco Bartolommeo Rastrelli. However, this was not the first winter residence of the tsar. The first Winter House of Peter I, a modest two-storey building, was erected in 1711 on the bank of the canal connecting the Moika and the Neva. The canal retained to our days and is known as the Winter Canal. Ten years later, the second Winter Palace was built after the project of the architect Mattarnovi. It stood on the place where the present-day Hermitage Theatre is situated. In 1727, the architect Domenico Trezzini

*enlarged the building and created the third
Winter Palace. However, Empress Anna
Ioannovna considered it to be too modest, and,
in 1730 she moved to the house of Admiral
Apraksin located not far from the contemporary
Palace Bridge. Five years later, the young
Francesco Bartolommeo Rastrelli re-built
Apraksin's house. It became the fourth Winter
Palace. The fifth Winter Palace was founded
on the place of the fourth one in 1754, as the
architect proved to Empress Elizabeth Petrovna
that a new winter palace was to be built. Some
thousands of the best Russian builders erected
a new palace under the supervision of Rastrelli.
By 1762 construction works were finished.*

the Small Hermitage adhering to it, while the western façade, concealing a small, charming garden, looks through the wide street onto the ancient Admiralty building. At this site, at the time of the erection of St. Petersburg in the early eighteenth century, palaces, the residences of dignitaries, as well as of the founder of the city, Emperor Peter I, stood. Empress Anna Ioannovna settled in one of them in the early of the 1730s. After her, her successors also lived here during the winters. Russian power grew and expanded; the might of Russian monarchs intensified and in 1754–62 at the site of the decayed old "Winter Residence", the chief architect of the Russian court, Francesco Bartholommeo Rastrelli, erected the new Winter Palace corresponding to the dignity and brilliance of the Russian autocracy.

The Small Hermitage

The 1917 revolution transformed the Imperial Hermitage into the State Hermitage. During the course of almost 80 years of the twentieth century the museum collections expanded almost fourfold. In the first years following the revolution the Hermitage received the most lavish private art collections, nationalized by the Soviet government. In the 1930s–1940s a series of Leningrad and Moscow museums were closed by the government; their collections, for example, French paintings of the nineteenth–twentieth centuries, found refuge in the Hermitage. A constant source of addi-

"My museum in the Hermitage consists, not counting pictures and the Raphael Loggias, of 38,000 books, four rooms filled with books and engravings, 10,000 carved stones, approximately 10,000 drawings and scientific objects occupying two large rooms", wrote Catherine II to Grimm in her letter of September 18, 1790.

Alexander Roslin. 1718–1793. Sweden.
Portrait of Catherine II. 1766–77

tions to the Hermitage were scientific, archaeological and collecting expeditions. Thus were amassed the collections of Scythian art and of ancient Altai art, old Russian icons, monuments of art from Central Asia, China and Tibet. Works of art, acquired through the Hermitage Purchasing Commission, at international auctions and presented by collectors and contemporary artists, merged with the Hermitage collection.

Side by side with the departments already established as far back as the eighteenth and nineteenth centuries—the Departments of Western European Art, the Ancient World and Numismatics—in 1920 and 1931 the Oriental Department and Department of Archaeology were founded respectively, which were followed by the Department of the History of Russian Culture in 1941.

The Hermitage did not remain aside from the terrible ordeals which befell Russia's lot in the twentieth century. At the end of the 1920s–early 1930s the museum lost a part of its treasures. According to the shortsighted decree of the government they were sold to foreign buyers. More than fifty works of art, Raphael's *Madonna Alba*, Titian's *Venus with a Mirror*, Rubens' portraits of Isabella Brant and Elena Fourmen (the renowned *Fur Coat*), Rembrandt's *Portrait of Titus*, Watteau's *Mezzetin* and a series of others, are now in the museums of Europe and the United States.

During the years of the Second World War the Hermitage experienced all the tribulations of Leningrad's 900-day blockade. As early as the commencement of the Great Patriotic War (1941–1945) the museum's most prized collections were evacuated to Sverdlovsk (Yekaterinburg) in the Urals accompanied by their curators. The museum employees who remained in the Hermitage courageously attempted to safeguard the exhibits remaining there from bombs, shelling and from the dampness of deserted halls and buildings. Dying from hunger in the besieged city, scholars from the Hermitage did not cease their research work.

The war ended, the collections were brought back from evacuation, and the restored halls began to radiate beauty. Already more than fifty years have passed from that tragic time. The Hermitage lives the routine life of a large museum: it collects, safeguards and studies the relics of world art and organizes exhibitions.

Portico of the New Hermitage

The growing art collection needed new rooms. Nicholas I commissioned the German architect Leo von Klenze to design a new building for a museum. In 1838 the Emperor while visiting Germany happened to see in Munich the Glyptotheka and Pinacotheca built after the design of this architect. The erection of the new museum after Leo von Klenze's project was fulfilled by the Russian architects Vasily Stasov and Nikolai Yefimov. The ten five-metres high figures of atlantes decorating the museum's portico were made by the sculptor Alexander Terebenev.

9

The allegorical statue of the Sovereignity
The statue was transferred from
the Taurida Palace.

The Jordan Staircase

The two rows of white columns form a kind of
a gallery in the depth of which one can see the
wide flight of the Main Staircase. It is flooded
with light and is glittering with gilt ornaments.
Russian modellers, carvers and gilders realized
Rastrelli's fantasies in stone, marble, wood and
even in plaster of Paris. While restoring the Main
Staircase after the fire of 1837 Stasov managed
to retain Rastrelli's majestic conception though
he introduced some new decorative elements.
The statues of Athena with a spear in her hand,
Hermes in a winged cap, Flora with flowers and
Femide with a sword and scales in her hands
were placed along the walls of the staircase.
The fascinating moulding decorating the Jordan
Staircase was made by hand. At first the contour
of a future decor was traced by a sharp tool on
the plain wall. Then alabaster or plaster of Paris
was put on the place, and after that the decor
was modelled. Modellers worked without
previously made moulds, so no ornament is an
exact copy of others. The moulding decorating
the palace's façades was made by the same way.
Gilding was a rather laborious process too: the
modelled ornament was covered with a special
varnish which, after it had hardened, formed a
smooth surface. This process was repeated twice.
Then the gilding began. Only pure gold was used.
It was kept in the form of most thin leaves in
special books. The gold leaf was carefully blown
up on a suede pillow from which, with a little fan
made of hair from the squirrel tail, the leaf was
transferred on the modelled ornament to which
it stuck. Then it was polished with a soft brush in
order to receive a smooth and glittering surface.

Thousands of visitors from all corners of the globe visit the
Hermitage every year. For them the journey to the realm of
treasures of world culture begins at the Winter Palace.
However, Rastrelli did not succeed in completing the palace
interior decoration. After him several generations of the most
illustrious architects worked on the decoration of its interiors. Only several rooms preserve the magnificent Baroque
character conceived by Rastrelli. Above all, the Main Staircase.
Already from afar, from the entrance gallery, its first steps are
visible leading to the statue *Allegory of the State (Sovereignty)*
on the lower landing. When having walked up to it, suddenly
you emerge from the semi-darkness of the vaults into a
brightly illuminated vast space spanning the entire height of
the building. There, on the height of almost 22 metres,
Olympic gods soar in a blue sky of the painted ceiling, light
pours through the windows and glides along the white walls
with its gilt ornamentation and the statues of gods and mus-
es. The white marble staircase with its carved balustrade leads
into the state halls. In the eighteenth century it was called
the Ambassadorial Staircase, and in the nineteenth century,
the Jordan Staircase: during the winter, at the Epiphany, a
holiday procession descended along it to the "Jordan font"
cut through the ice on the Neva, where they bathed thus
recalling the Baptism of Christ.

Big Coach. France. 18th century

*The Peter (the Small Throne) Hall in
the Winter Palace*

*The vaults of the hall are painted with gold
patterns consisting of crowns, two-headed eagles
and the PP (Peter Primus) monograms. The
official allegorical portrait of Peter I where he
is represented accompanied by Minerva is to
symbolize military successes of the Russian State.
The portrait "Peter I with the Allegorical Figure
of Minerva" (between 1732–34) was painted
by the Venetian artist Jacopo Amiconi. The
emperor's throne standing on the dais under the
picture was made after Peter's death in England
in 1731 by Nicholas Clausen of fumed oak and
decorated with gilded silver. On the upper part
of the walls there are depictions of the battles
won by Peter I: the Poltava Battle and the Battle
at Lesnaya.*

Two suites of main halls lead from the Main Staircase; one
along the Neva, the other, the Great Suite of reception halls,
leads into the depth of the palace. The Great Suite was created from the mid-eighteenth century to the close of the 1830s
by the best architects of Russian Classicism. Vasily Stasov,
who restored the halls after the fire of December 1837,
deserves especially great commendation. He restored the
appearance which had been conceived by his predecessors,
bringing slight alterations to it corresponding to contemporary tastes. The suite of halls opens onto the Fieldmarshals
Hall. Officers of the guard were on duty here, and the mounting of the palace guard also took place here. At that time
portraits of Russian fieldmarshals hung on the walls.

The theme of martial glory, might and the majesty of the
Russian Empire was central in the design of the palace official halls. It also is realized in the decoration of the neighbouring Memorial Room of Peter the Great. It is dedicated to
the memory of Peter the Great, the first emperor of Russia.
Peter is presented accompanied by Minerva in Jacopo
Amigoni's painting in the niche of the hall; the emperor's
throne is beneath the painting. Everywhere—in frescoes, in
velvet wall panels embroidered in silver—the coat-of-arms of
Peter I, the state arms of the Russian Empire and laurel
wreathes are present. The decor of the Armorial Hall embod-
ies the unity of the empire. The chandeliers of this vast hall
covering an area of 1,000 metres are ornamented with
shields with the coat-of-arms of Russian gubernias. Here the
emperor met his subjects, received the deputies of Russia's
cities and the representatives of all the estates—the nobility,
merchants and city dwellers.

The 1812 War Gallery in the Winter Palace

The gallery was built in 1826 as a memorial to the heroic victory of Russian arm in the Patriotic War of 1812 against Napoleon. The walls bear the names of the places where heroic battles of Russian and French armies took place: Borodino, Tarutino, Krasnoye, Paris and many others. Armour and allegorical female figures holding laurel wreaths decorate the hall. The 332 portraits of Russian generals hanging in the gallery were painted by the English portraitist George Dawe and the Russian artists Vasily Golike and Alexander Poliakov. The generals sat for the artists in the studio arranged in one of the palace rooms. Who could not come and pose had to send their representations to the artists. If the hero was killed in the battle or died after the wounds his representation nevertheless had to be sent in order the artists could depict his image for future generations.

The Coat-of-Arms Hall in the Winter Palace

The huge Coat-of-Arms Hall with its area of 1,000 m² was intended for ceremonial receptions. The architect Stasov decorated it with gilt Corinthian columns. The bronze chandeliers, adorned with shields bearing relief representations of the arms of Russian gubernias were installed later. According to the first project of Rastrelli part of the present-day Coat-of-Arms Hall was occupied with the ceremonial Light, or New, Gallery. The gallery joined the Jordan Staircase and the Great Church. In 1775 the architect Yuri Velten made it almost twice wider. It was after that when the Coat-of-Arms Hall received the name of the White Hall. It was decorated with moulded and carved Classical ornaments, vase-shaped lamps and statues made by the remarkable Russian sculptor Fiodor Gordeyev.

Next to the Armorial Hall is the Gallery of the Patriotic War of 1812, dedicated to Russia's victory over Napoleon's armies. 332 portraits of Russian generals who participated in this war hang on its walls. The official portrait of Emperor Alexander I, under a canopy, hangs separately. A portrait of the Commander-in-Chief of the Russian Army, Mikhail Kutuzov, hangs in the honoured place before the entrance to the Great Throne Hall.

The Great Throne Hall, or the St. George Hall, is the most majestic and solemn hall of the palace. It is decorated with snow-white Carrara marble, set off with gilded bronze bases and capitals of the columns, cornices and the balusters of the balconies. The plated bronze ornamentation of the ceiling is mirrored in the parquet patterns, composed of sixteen different kinds of valuable woods. St. George slaying the Dragon— an ancient Russian state emblem personifying the might of Russia—is depicted over the site where the emperor's throne used to stand. The most important state acts and great receptions took place there.

They were preceded as a rule by a service in the adjoining Great Church of the Winter Palace, which has preserved its Baroque decoration. In our day eighteenth-century Western European china is housed here.

The main halls are used for displaying the exhibits: for example, the lavishly gilded and painted Great Carriage, created in the early eighteenth century, by commission of Peter I, in Paris, is kept in the Fieldmar-shals Hall. It was used for Catherine II's outings during her coronation in Moscow in 1763. Similar carriages and coaches of the palace Carriage Coach-yard now comprise one of the most interesting collections in the Hermitage.

The suite of state rooms along the Neva consists of three halls. The small Antechamber is decorated witha malachite rotunda, the work of nineteenth-century stone-cutters from the Urals. It was transferred here from the Cathedral of Our Lady of Kazan after the 1917 revolution.

From the Ante-chamber the entrance leads to the Great, or St. Nicholas Hall, and then to the Concert Hall. The St. Nicholas Hall is the largest hall in the palace with an area of over 1,103 square metres. Court balls were held there, where up to 3,000 guests gathered.

The silver sepulchre of Alexander Nevsky, the Russian thirteenth-century prince and military leader, is kept in the Concert Hall. It was transferred to the Hermitage from the Alexander Nevsky Monastery. At one time the guests invited to a ball or a reception waited there for the ceremonial exit of the imperial family from the inner, private chambers.

The sepulchre of Holy Prince Alexander Nevsky

By the order of Empress Elizabeth Petrovna, in 1746, the creation of the sepulchre of Prince Alexander Nevsky began. It was made of the silver from the Kolyvansko-Voskresensky mine. The monumental sepulchre is one of brilliant examples of the applied arts of the 18th century. The sepulchre consists of a large sarcophagus, large fife-tiered pyramid, two pedestals decorated with representations of armour and a pair of candle-sticks. The sarcophagus by the feet of the central pyramid is decorated with the chased scenes illustrating the most important episodes in Alexander Nevsky's campaigns. Mikhail Lomonosov's verse glorifying Alexander Nevsky, Peter I and Elizabeth Petrovna to whose order this monument was erected is engraved on one of the sepulchre's side. In the centre of the pyramid, is a bas-relief with an allegorical representation of Faith directing Alexander Nevsky.

Boudoir in the Winter Palace

The round passage hall, the Rotunda, unites the great Imperial part of the palace with the remaining living palatial quarters. The private entrance of Her Imperial Majesty leads to the state White Hall and Gold Drawing-Room of Empress Maria Alexandrovna, consort of Alexander II. Adjoining it, are the Green Dining-Room and the Study, upholstered with crimson damask, which frequently served for musical evenings. Further are the private chambers, the Boudoir and the Blue Bedroom.

The great imperial private chambers acquired their shape towards the outset of the nineteenth century. Alexander I and his spouse were the first to live there. After the 1837 fire the architect Alexander Briullov, who was entrusted with the restoration of the palatial living rooms, decorated these chambers for empress Alexandra Fiodorovna, the consort of Nicholas I, anew. The splendid decor of the Malachite Drawing-Room has been preserved to our day. This room with its windows looking onto the Neva seem dazzlingly elegant thanks to the green malachite from the Urals which revetted the columns, fireplaces and tables. It harmonizes marvellously with the white walls, gilding, with the crimson upholstery of the furniture and draperies and with the patterned parquet.

The Malachite Drawing-Room in the Winter Palace

The columns in the room are faced with malachite of bright and tender green tones. The green colour of the malachite, the gilt moulding of the ceiling and doors, as well as white walls and the crimson silk of the furniture match wonderfully. This room was decorated by the architects Alexander Briullov and Vasily Stasov. Malachite as decorative stone was known from ancient times and was widely used in Russia. There are on exhibit in this room many items of this delicate and costly mineral: vases, tables, caskets, paper-weights and many others. Every article of malachite was made by a special device. The mould of stone, copper or any other material was covered with hot mastic and then malachite plates several millimetres thick were glued on. In the result, the master had to achieve an impression that the article is made of a monolith. If there are little clinks between the plates, they were to be filled with mastic mixed with malachite powder. The article was polished and the natural pattern of the malachite seemed to be undisturbed. This method became known as "Russian mosaics".

The Gothic Library (Nicholas II's library) in the Winter Palace

The Small Dining-Room in the Winter Palace

The walls of the room are decorated with tapestries and hand-woven carpets produced in the 18th century at the St. Petersburg Tapestry Manufacture which worked to the orders from tsar palaces and the Hermitage. Besides tapestries, the eighteenth-century crystal chandelier of English make decorates the Small Dining-Room. In the lower part of the chandelier, inside a mirror ball, a musical instrument playing some English songs is hidden.

The last Russian emperor, Nicholas II, ordered the greater part of the rooms of the private imperial quarters to be redesigned in his taste—simply, and comfortably. In our day the Library of Nicholas II has been preserved, as well as the Private Dining Room of the Emperor's family decorated in the eighteenth-century French Rococo style.

The Provisional Government under Alexander Kerensky was quartered in these rooms after the fall of the monarchy in 1917. Members of the government were arrested in the Private Dining-Room on October 26, 1917, during the night of the October coup d'etat.

The idea of the creation of a "Hermitage" belonged to the first proprietress of the Winter Palace, Catherine II. This French word—*hermite* means "the abode of a recluse", or "a place of solitude". In the eighteenth century it was used to designate secluded studies or park pavilions, where a selected social set gathered surrounded by pictures and rare objets d'art. Catherine decreed that a small building next to the Winter Palace should be built, which later was called the Small Hermitage. The Empress' first collections were kept in its Northern Pavilion, erected in 1767–69 by Jean-Baptiste Vallin de la Mothe. Her guests attended "small" Hermitage receptions in the small study. In accordance with etiquette for guests, composed by the hostess herself, the former were prescribed "to leave behind the doors, uniformly, all ranks, as well as hats and, in particular, rapiers", "to be gay", "to eat with relish and to drink to measure..."

The Gold Drawing-Room in the Winter Palace

The beginning of the wonderful collection of carved precious and coloured stones was laid by Empress Catherine II. She was very fond of these miniature masterpieces and used to call this fondness her "stone illness".
The art of glyptic fascinated collectors from time immemorial. Depictions on stones were carved by hand or with the help of the lathe known in Greece as early as the 6th century B.C.

*The Gonzaga cameo. Alexandria.
3rd century B.C.*

*Cameos, i.e. pieces of stone with a relief depiction,
were mounted into diadems, fibulae and rings
and were considered to be works of art. The
Gonzaga cameo is one of the largest. Its
dimensions are 15.7 x 11.8 cm. Two profiles are
carved in high relief on the piece of three-layered
sardonyx. They belong to Ptolemy II Philadelphus
and his spouse, Arsinoë. This wonderful cameo is
made in the 3rd century B.C. in Alexandria, the
capital of Egypt. Its history can be traced back to
the 16th century, when it belonged to Isabella
D'Este, wife of Gonzaga, the Herzog of Mantua.
Hence its name. Later it occured in the collection
of Josephine Beauharnais who presented it to the
Russian tsar, Alexander I.*

*Constantine the Great and Tyche of
Constantinople. Cameo. 4th century. Rome*

*This cameo is referred to the decline of the
Antique World. Tyche, or Fortune, in antique
mythology is the goddess of happiness, a
patroness of cities.*

The Pavilion Hall in the Small Hermitage

Its columns supporting a light gallery with rounded balconies and the shell-shaped fountains near the walls resemble the inner courts of Eastern shakhs' palaces.The floor in the Pavilion Hall is decorated with a mosaic panel made of smalt. The mosaic panel is a copy of an ancient Roman mosaic panel found at the excavations in the environs of Rome. The copy was done by Russian artists.

The panel represents scenes from Antique mythology. In the centre, there is a depiction of the head of the Medusa Gorgon. It is surrounded with scenes depicting the fights of Greeks and centaurs. Fantastic sea creatures, such as Nereids and Tritons, are represented along the edges of the composition. This copy of an Ancient Rome mosaic panel was made and brought to St. Petersburg in the 1850s. One can find there some other articles decorated with mosaic panels: tables with table-tops featuring wonderful examples of the Italian nineteenth-century mosaics. Once, part of the Pavilion Hall was occupied with a small dining-room adjoining some other rooms and the winter garden where, in tubs, evergreens grew, singing birds from Southern countries, monkeys and squirrels lived. One of these small rooms served as a dining-room. Its table, with the help of a special device was lowered down to the kitchen where it was laid and then lifted back to the room. It was done in order not to disturb the entertainments of the empress and her guests.

One large Pavilion Hall, created in the 1850s, is to be found here today. Bright and elegant, it is decorated with passage galleries, arcades and sparkling crystal chandeliers. The fountains near the walls let fall drops of water, recalling the Fountain of Tears of the Crimean khan's palace at Bakhchiserai. The floor is covered with copies of a mosaic floor of an ancient Roman bath. The Peacock Clock of an English eighteenth-century make, with moving figures of birds, which had been acquired by Catherine II, is displayed there now. The windows look out onto the Hanging Garden of the "Russian Semiramis". It was laid out on the volutes of the lower floor in 1764–69.

Rogier van der Weyden. 1400–1464. The Netherlands.
St. Luke Painting a Portrait of the Virgin

Robert Campin. C. 1380–1444.
The Netherlands. The Virgin and Child by
the Fireside. Right wing of a diptych

A contemporary of the Van Eyk brothers,
founders of the Renaissance in the Netherlands,
Robert Campin depicted the Virgin in a modest-
looking interior. At the first glance, the picture
seems to represent a genre scene, so scrupulous
was the painter in depiction of objects of
everyday life. However these details were
perceived by contemporaries as symbols.
For example, the basin, ewer and the white
towl are symbols of innocence and purity
of the Virgin Mary.

Flanking it, between the Northern and Southern pavilions, galleries were built for Catherine's growing collection in 1768–75. Even today they serve for displaying exhibitions. Now the exposition of Medieval Western European applied arts (5th–15th centuries)—church vessels, reliquaries, bronze watercarriers, enamels, china, stained-glass panels and tapestries—is on display here. The exhibition of the fifteenth- and sixteenth-centuries Netherland art, small but providing a sufficiently full representation of the leading artists of Old Netherland painting, such as for example, Robert Campin, Rogier Van der Weyden, Hugo van der Goes and Lucas van Leyden, is also displayed there.

Pieter Brueghel the Younger. C. 1564–1638. The Netherlands.
St. John the Baptist Preaching. 1604

Pieter Brueghel the Younger. C. 1564–1638. The Netherlands.
The Adoration of the Magi

In 1771–87 Yuri Velten built the Great (Old) Hermitage next
to the Small Hermitage. The passage leads straight from the
Pavilion Hall of the Small Hermitage to the Main Staircase of
the Old Hermitage. It had been already built in the mid-nineteenth century when the State Council was located on the
ground floor and to this day its name Sovetskaya (Council)
has been preserved.

The staircase enclosed with open-worked cast-iron railings
connects the vestibule with the upper landing decorated
with sculptures, mosaic tables and a large vase of Ural malachite, a Russian nineteenth-century work. The entrance to
the halls of the first floor is located here. In the eighteenth
century they were a continuation of Catherine II's Hermitage.
She organized "large" Hermitage receptions here, where up
to 200 guests gathered. Her collections were also housed
here. In the 1850s they were transferred to the New
Hermitage, which had just been erected, and the abandoned

*Painters and sculptors played an important role
in the origin of the Renaissance culture in Italy.
The country was separated into independent
cities-states and, as a result, many artistic
schools were formed in Italy: the Florentine,
Roman, Venetian and others. The Florentine
school is represented in the Hermitage by a large
number of pictures. Though there are no picture
by Mazacco and Donatello, rare artists beyond
Italy, nevertheless one of the most active art
school of the medieval Italy is represented in the
Hermitage brightly enough. However differ the
works of Fra Angelico and Sandro Botticelli,
marbles by Antonio Rosselino and Desiderio da
Settigniano, the common criteria for all of them
are the value of earthly being, belief in beauty
and boundless possibilities of the harmonious
human being.*

Of few paintings by Leonardo da Vinci retained to our time, two are in the Hermitage. "The Madonna and Child" ("The Litta Madonna") was finished, when the artist had probably moved to Milan. The artistic principles of the High Renaissance are already revealed here to full extent. Everything inessential is missed here.

The dark neutral background makes it possible to concentrate the viewer's attention on the figures constituting a steady and harmonious group. The profundity and nobility of the content are harmoniously combined in the picture with clear logics of the composition and virtuosity of execution. The windows symmetrically located on the both sides of the Madonna and Child underline the balanced character of the composition, while the natural ties of people and nature are emphasized with the endless mountainous landscape behind the windows.

rooms were once again redecorated by Andrei Stakenschneider for the heir to the throne. In our day the exhibition of the Italian Renaissance art (13th–16th centuries) is housed here. It begins with the Hall of the Primitives, i.e. the Protorenaissance art (13th–14th centuries), where the *Madonna* by Simone Martini belonging to the fourteenth-century Siennese School occupies a special place. This is the right fold of the diptych from the *Annunciation*; its left fold is in the National Gallery in Washington.

The most famous part of the collection comprises the works of the great sixteenth-century Italian masters. The museum's jewel are the two pictures by Leonardo da Vinci (1452–1519) (out of not more than fourteen works remaining in the world). *The Benois Madonna*, purchased from the Benois family in St. Petersburg in 1914, was executed by the young Leonardo in 1478 in Florence. Through it he realized his knowledge of nature and man. His young Madonna playing

Giorgione. 1478–1510. Italy.
Judith

This picture entered the Hermitage as part of the Crozat collection. Hard negotiations with the heirs of the baron lasted for a year and half and resulted that the Hermitage collection was enriched with wonderful pieces of painting, this picture being one of them. The acquisition of the Crozat collection caused a sensation in Europe not by the fact that such an artistic treasure left Paris, but by the fact of purchasing such a costly collection at the time when Russia was at the height of the war of 1770–71.

with Her earnest and inquisitive son, incarnates the earthly beauty, youth and maternal joy. Acquired in 1865 in Italy from Count Litta, *The Litta Madonna*, in contrast, is the mature work of the artist, created in 1490 in Milan. The harmonic ideal of beauty of the Renaissance epoch is realized in the image of the inspired, beautiful woman, with a child in her arms. Both paintings are exhibited separately in a state hall. The adjoining gallery houses paintings of the Venetian Renaissance School. Here one can admire Giorgione's enigmatic and magnificent *Judith* and nine pictures of the great Titian. Among them *Danaë*, *The Penitent Magdalene*, celebrating the charm and lofty fervency of feminine sentiments, and *St. Sebastian*, the well-known late artist's work.

The Raphael Loggias evoke still yet another genius of the Renaissance—a copy of the Vatican palace loggias painted by Raphael and his pupils in the early sixteenth century. In 1780–87 Raphael's frescoes were copied on canvas by order of Catherine II, brought to St. Petersburg and mounted on the volutes and walls of the gallery, specially built by Giacomo Quarenghi to the south of the Old Hermitage. Illuminated with light from the high windows, reflected in the mirrors, the gallery, with its semicircular arches, measuredly following one another, charms one with the pure and joyful colours of whimsical arabesque patterns. Paintings on Biblical themes, the renowned *Bible of Raphael*, are icluded in its decor. The neighbouring hall contains two pictures painted by Raphael himself.

The Conestabile Madonna is especially famous, and was acquired by Emperor Alexander II for his spouse, Empress Maria Alexandrovna, in 1870 from the Conestabile family in Perugia. This small tondo is set into a gilded frame created after Raphael's drawing. Standing against the background of a springtime landscape, a slightly sorrowful Madonna, with the Infant in her arms, seems an incarnation of purity and tenderness. The collection of Italian ceramics—more than 500 magnificent examples of Faenza, Urbino, Deruta and Castel-Durante ceramics—is also on exhibit here.

Italian majolica of the 16th century

On the walls of the adjoining hall are copies of Raphael's Vatican frescoes created by his pupils. The Crouching Boy by the great Michelangelo, intended for the unfinished decoration of the Medici tomb in Florence, stands in the centre of the hall.

The Raphael Loggias, the halls with his pictures and frescoes of his school, comprise a part of the New Hermitage. It was built in 1842–51 as a proper museum building by Vasily Stasov and Nikolai Yefimov after a project by leo von Klenze, who designed the Munich Pinakothek. On February 5, 1852, the Imperial Public Museum was solemnly opened in the New Hermitage. In the early years of its existence visits to the museum were strictly regulated by the office of the Court Ministry. Visitors were admitted only in uniforms, tail-coats and court attire. But as early as the 1860s entrance to the museum became free. The museum worked daily apart from holidays and those hours when "His Imperial Majesty deigned to visit the Hermitage". The entrance to the museum was from quiet Millionnaya Street through the portico with the figures of ten granite atlantes. The vestibule of the Main Staircase, solemn and austere like the entrance to a temple, was behind it. Its walls were revetted with stucco imitating yellow marble, and twenty monolithic columns of grey granite towered above.

Raphael (Raffaello Santi). 1483–1520. Italy. The Conestabile Madonna. C. 1503

This picture commissioned by Count Alfano da Diamente in the late 18th century became the property of the Conestabile family from which it was bought in 1870. This is one of the earliest representations of the Madonna which brought glory to Raphael. His elevated, purified of everything trivial and casual images have no prototype. The delicate spring landscape echoes to the pure face of the Madonna. "In order to paint a beautiful woman I ought to have seen a lot of beautiful women, but, as really beautiful women and judges are few, I take as my guide a certain idea", the artist wrote. While transferring the picture from the panel on the canvas made by the Hermitage restorers in 1881 for better preservation of the picture they discovered that originally the painter, following his teacher Perugino, depicted a pomegranate in the Madonna's hand. Later he changed it for a book. The wonderfully carved frame of the picture is of great interest too. It is considered to be made after the design by Raphael. Before the picture was transferred on the canvas, it constituted a single whole with the picture.

*Shield, helmet and a gountlet. 16th century.
Italy*

*As a rule, pieces of armour had a sophisticated
ornament. Metal was coloured while tempering,
and decor was formed of a thin gold thread that
filled the hollows. The armour was rather heavy,
from 40 up to 80 kilogrammes and cost very
much.*

Dagger. 16th century. Italy

*The Renaissance ceremonial dagger was part
of a set of ceremonial arms produced in Iran,
Turkey, Indonesia and Italy and was kept in a
special casket which was housed in the private
rooms of Peter I.*

The Knight Hall in the New Hermitage

*Various pieces of West European battle, tourna-
ment and hunting armour, both cold steel and
firearms, are represented in the Khight Hall.
One of the most wonderful items is the "Gothic
armour" made in Augsburg in the first half of
the 15th century by Lorenz Helmschmidt. It
protected almost the whole body of a knight with
movable metal plates. Such an armour weighed
16-20 kilogrammes averagely. But it was not all
the weight the knight had to bear. One must add
the weight of the hauberk worn under armour
and the weight of arms. The knight of that period
was armed with one-hand and additional, "one-
and-half-hand" swords, a lance more than three
metres long, a battle axe and hammer or a
mace. The "cavalcade of knights" located in
the hall demonstrates armour protecting horses
as well.*

The halls on the ground floor, built for the keeping of ancient relics, now house the exhibitions of the Department of the Ancient World. The Twenty-Columned Hall, divided, like an ancient Greek temple, into three naves with granite columns, meant for collections of antique vases. The slender black-lacquered hydria from the 4th century B.C. from the town of Cumae, displayed here, was called the Queen of the Vases ("Regina vasorum"). On its dainty shouldewrs and grooved body there are delicately modelled reliefs, depicting Hellenic mysteries and a procession of wild beasts. This is one of the masterpieces in the collection of antique ceramics, which includes around 15,000 Ancient Greek, Etruscan and Italic vases.

Pottery in Greece was not only the product for export but it became a kind of arts. More than a hundred types of clay vessels of different shapes are known.

Antique forms are imitated by Russian stone-carvers in their huge jasper vase weighing 19 tons, made in the Kolyvan Factory in the Altai mountains in 1831–43. The Kolyvan Vase adorns one of the halls of classical Roman art.

The Twenty-Columned Hall
in the New Hermitage

The architects while constructing the New Hermitage were striving to imitate the architecture of Ancient Greece. Some halls of the museum had to resemble Greek temples or houses. Such is the Twenty-Columned Hall. The two rows of columns of gray granite divide it into three naves, the central one being narrower than the side ones. Such a device was characteristic for Greek and Roman temples. The side walls are decorated with bright pictures depicting scenes from antique myths. Like in Greek and especially in Roman temples, the floor in the hall is composed of small square pieces of white, yellow, gray, black and dark-red marble forming beautiful mosaic panels. These marble pieces were produced at the Peterhof Grinding Factory.

Youth Reclining. Etruria. 4th century B.C.

This urn in the shape of a reclining youth was found in an Etruscan necropolis near Perugia in 1842.

The Cumae vase "Regina Vasorum". 4th century B.C. Italy

Exposition of Roman sculpture in the New Hermitage

A rich collection of Ancient Roman marble sculpture is displayed in the halls, designed in the traditions of classical architecture. Conceived as a peristyle hall with sculpture, it recreates an inner courtyard of a Roman house. The collection of Roman sculptural portraits is especially famed; it includes about 120 pieces. A brilliant, slightly tired of life, young patrician, emperor Lucius Verus; an unknown, refined woman, nicknamed the "Syrian Woman", who is submerged in the world of complex moods; and many other pieces are presented in the works of this collection.

Portrait of Decimus Caelius Calvinus Balbinus, Roman Emperor. 3rd century

Dionysus and Cora. Roman copy of a Hellenistic original

Once this sculptural group used to decorate the Grotto by the pond in the Catherine Park in Tsarskoye Selo.

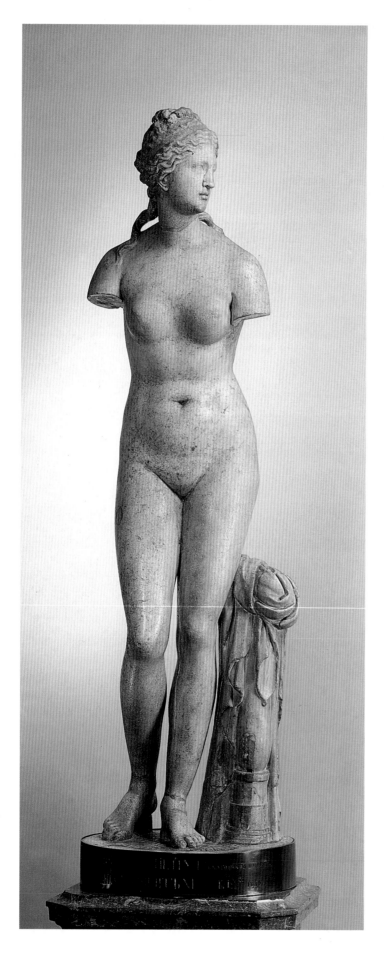

*Venus of Taurida. Roman copy of
the 1st–2nd centuries of the Greek original
of the 3rd century B.C.*

In 1718, Peter I sent from Amsterdam to Italy his
agent, Kologrivov, to purchase there works of art.
Besides paintings, the emperor was interested in
acquiring antique statues. It was a very difficult
task because the Pope banned the removal of
antique sculpture from the Roman Province.
The purchasing in 1719 of the statue of Venus
was on the eve of break, and only long-lasting
and hard negotiations made it possible to bring
the statue to Russia. The statue received the
name of the Venus of Taurida for it was
transferred to the Hermitage from the Taurida
Palace, the splendid residence of Prince
Potiomkin.

*Heracles Fighting the Nemean Lion.
Roman copy of the 1st–2nd centuries of the
original by Lysippus*

This small-sized sculptural group of marble is a
diminished replica of the bronze original by
Lysippus. The Lysippus' sculpture "Heracles
Fighting the Nemean Lion" was one in the series
of sculptures made for the city of Alisia in
Acarnania and devoted to the twelve labours
of Heracles. The sculptor represented the peak
of the fight when the hero is strangling the lion
with his might hands. The figures are sophisticat-
edly turned, as the sculpture was intended to be
seen from all sides. Lysippus was the sculptor
who crowned the best achievements of the Greek
art of the 5th–4th centuries B.C.

Twenty centuries of the history of Ancient glyptics is reflected in the exhibition of gems, one of the best collections in the world. Its jewel, the Gonzaga Cameo (3rd century B.C.)—a double portrait of the Alexandrian Emperor Ptolemeus and his consort, Arsinoë, carved of a three-layered sardonyx. Being kept in the palace of Duke of Mantua, the cameo later turned up in the collection of Josephine Beauharnais, who then presented it to Russian Emperor Alexander I.

A separate part of the exhibition is dedicated to the culture of the cities of the Northern Black Sea cost, founded by the Greeks in the 7th–6th centuries B.C. Russian archaeologists brought remarkable relics of ancient sculpture and handicrafts from there. In the burial-mound of Kul-Oba near Kerch gold pendants from the 5th century B.C. were discovered. The head of the famous statue of Athena of Parthenos by the great Athenian sculptor Pheidias was reproduced on the medallion.

Ear-rings. Greece. 4th century B.C.

The disk of each ear-ring is decorated with several rows of granulas, and their inner side is covered with sophisticated filigreed patterns. The boat is suspended on two chains with vegetable patterns. The central scene depicts a quadriga dashing at full speed. If is driven by Nike, the goddess of victory. A youth with a shield stands by her side. The composition is crowned by figures of winged eroses. The central group is so small (width, 1.2 cm; height, 1.1 cm) that these ear-rings are considered to be an example of Greek microtechnique.

*Gold vessel decorated with the depiction
of Scythian warriors. Greece. 4th century B.C.*

Soldiers mining stones in the steppe near Kerch
in 1830 found a rich burial place under the
mound of Kul-Oba what means in Tatarian "the
mound of ashes". Three men were buried there:
a noble warrior, his wife and armour-bearer.
The researchers who studied this burial place
referred it to the 4th century B.C., and because
of numerous splendid gold things of Greek make
found there they presumed that it was the burial
place of the Bosporus ruler. All gold things from
this mound, the gold vase with the depiction
of Scythian warriors, grivna (neck decoration)
adorned with mounted Scythians, gold bowl,
arms mounted in gold, jewelry (ear-rings,
pendants, bracelets) were transferred to the
Hermitage and are now housed in a special
store-room, constituting part of the collection of
the Greek jewelry.

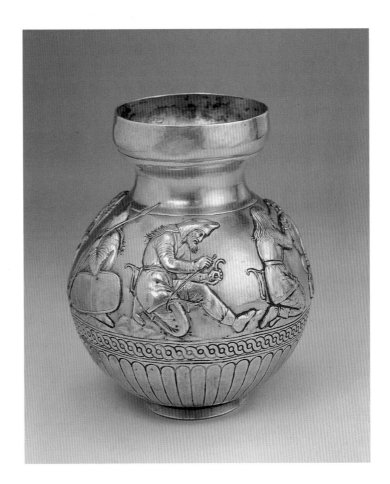

Comb. Late 5th–early 4th centuries B.C.

The Hermitage Scythian collection is the richest
in the world. In 1912–13, to the south of
Nikopol, in the region where in ancient time the
so-called "tsar Scythians", the most strong and
influential among other Scythian tribes, lived, a
burial place of a Scythian chief was excavated in
the Solokha mound. Besides typically Scythian
articles, such as a gold mounting of a sword, gold
plates, an outstanding piece of Greek jewelry
was found. It is known now as the "Solokha
comb". A great amount of objects of Greek make
in Scythian burial places testifies to broad trade
links of Greek towns with Scythia. In exchange
for slaves and grain Greeks gave various goods,
the objects of luxury occupying not the last place
among them. The tastes of Scythian nobility were
taken into consideration. So, the handle of the
comb is decorated with an expressive group of
Scythian warriors. The wholeness and expres-
siveness of the silhouette make it possible to see
in this comb a work from the mature style of the
Greek art of the Classic epoch and refer it to the
late 5th–early 4th centuries B.C.

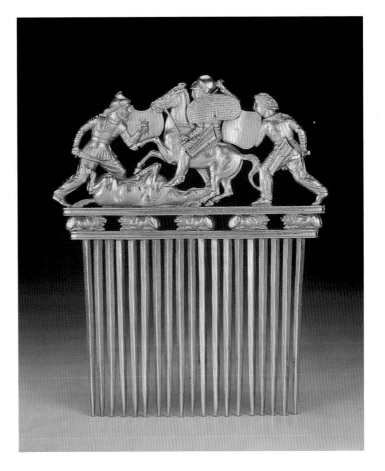

Antonio Canova. 1757–1822. Italy.
Cupid's Kiss

Gallery of History of the Old Painting
in the New Hermitage

Near the central rooms of the New Hermitage,
the Small and Large Skylights, the Gallery of the
History of Old Painting is situated. According to
the architect's project it had to serve as an
introduction into the rooms where West
European works of art were demonstrated. 86
pictures illustrate the history of old painting. They
are executed in the mid-19th century in the
technique imitating antique painting.

The first floor of the New Hermitage was specially designed
for a picture gallery. The entrance to it is from the Main
Staircase through the Gallery of the History of Old Painting
exhibiting the pictures on its walls recreating Ancient Greek
painting. They were created after the descriptions in ancient
texts in the encaustic technique, i.e. with wax paints upon
warmed up copper boards. The gallery, painted with antique
patterns, is adorned with malachite vases. The exhibition of
the 18th- to the early 19th-century West European sculpture

Caravaggio. 1571–1610. Italy.
The Lute Player. C. 1595

The Large Skylights in the New Hermitage

According to the project of the architect Leo von Klenze, the first floor of the museum was intended to house works of painting. The large halls were illuminated by natural light through their glass ceilings. It was done so that the pictures hanging on the walls might be evenly illuminated. The high ceilings of the halls are decorated with gilt moulding and medallions with portraits of renowned artists, sculptors and architects. Huge vases and different tables of various coloured stones, articles of malachite from the Urals and lazurite from the Pamirs are on exhibit in these rooms too. The gilt chairs, armchairs and sofas upholstered with red velvet were made at the palace works specially for the museum.

is to be found there. The works of the Italian sculptor Antonio Canova are especially alluring. One of his masterpieces is the marble group *The Three Graces*—the three beautiful companions of Venus: Beauty, Joy and Charm.

From reminiscences about ancient painting, the visitor goes on to Western European painting when entering the central halls of the Picture Gallery—the Skylights. These comprise three large halls, illuminated by natural light through glass ceilings. The pictures by Italian artists of the late 16th to the 18th centuries are exhibited there; they are a continuation of the exhibition of Italian art in the Old Hermitage. Here one can see Carravaggio's *The Lute Player* where the lyrical mood of the musician is brilliantly revealed.

Antonio Canaletto. 1697–1768. Italy.
Reception of the French Ambassador in Venice. 1740s

El Greco. 1541–1614. Spain.
The Apostles Peter and Paul. Between 1587–92

The third skylight houses the Spanish 15th-to early 19th-century masterpieces. The Apostle Peter radiating the warmth of Christian love and the passionate preacher Paul are presented in El Greco's painting. The limitless expanses of Spain unfold behind the back of St. Lawrence, ready to

endure martyrdom in the monumental canvas by Francisco de Zurbarán. There are two pictures belonging to the brush of Diego Velázquez—*Portrait of Count Olivares* and his youthful work, *Breakfast*, a vitally spontaneous, as well as symbolic, scene.

Francisco José de Goya. 1746–1828. Spain.
Portrait of Antonia Zárate. C. 1811

Diego Velázquez. 1599–1660. Spain.
Portrait of Count Olivares. C. 1640

61

Peter Paul Rubens. 1577–1640. Flanders.
Landscape with Rainbow. 1630s

A separate hall is dedicated to Peter Paul Rubens, the head and founder of a school. 42 of his paintings, from early to the final works, give a full and many-sided presentation of the "king of painters". One of his best pictures is *Perseus and Andromeda*, created in the 1620s. Rubens was then at the zenith of his glory, in love, felicitous: he had only just wedded to the delightful Elena Fourmen, the model of his captivating female images. The colour resounds triumphantly in the full mighty movement of the composition, glorifying the hero's valour, who received Andromeda's tender love as a recompense. *Portrait of a Lady-in-Waiting to the Infanta Isabella* charms one by the profusion of inner feelings on the young woman's visage. This is the traditional title of this famous portrait which might possibly be a portrayal of Rubens' daughter, who died early. It was executed on the basis of a drawing created in her lifetime and from the imagination of the artist, her father. One of Rubens' celebrated masterpieces, *Bacchus*, was painted at the end of his life. The Ancient god surrounded by his companions is the personification of the material, carnal origins of nature, almost burdening his corpulent body. The artist's sketches preserve the spontaneity of conception of the great painter, including those for the pictures belonging to the cycle *Life of Maria Medici* in the Louvre, Paris.

Ill. on pp. 64–65
Peter Paul Rubens. 1577–1640. Flanders.
Feast of Simon Pharisee

Ill. on pp. 66–67
Peter Paul Rubens. 1577–1640. Flanders.
Perseus and Andromeda. 1620s

Peter Paul Rubens. 1577–1640. Flanders.
Portrait of a Lady-in-Waiting to the Infanta Isabella. 1620s

Anthonis van Dyck. 1599–1641. Flanders.
Family Portrait. 1621

Twenty-four pictures by Anthonis van Dyck, the most independent pupil of Rubens, a famous European portraitist, cover the walls of an entire hall. Both chamber and magnificent official portraits painted at the English King's Court (*Portrait of Count Thomas Whorton*) are found here.

Anthonis van Dyck. 1599–1641. Flanders.
Self-Portrait. Late 1620s–early 1630s

Ill. on pp. 70–71
Anthonis van Dyck. 1599–1641. Flanders.
Rest on the Flight into Egypt (The Madonna with Partridges). 1630s

The Snyders Room in the New Hermitage

Five rooms of the New Hermitage are devoted to the exposition of the Flemish art of the 17th century. More than 500 pictures by almost of 140 artists constitute this collection, one of the best in the world.
Works by the outstanding master of the still life, Frans Snyders are a peculiar hymn to Nature. The huge canvases with the depictions of heaps of food once constituted a cycle intended to decorate the dining-room in the Bishop Palace in Brugge.

In the collection of paintings by Jacob Jordaens (1593–1678), who became the "leading painter of Antwerp" after Rubens, the widely famous *Bean King*, the colourful, rich depiction of a national Flemish celebration, takes pride of place. Still lifes by Frans Snyders, *Hunting Scene* by of Paul de Voos, and works by Teniers and Brouwer hang next to the paintings by Jordaens. The Dutch 17th- and 18th-century school of painting is presented in no less comprehensive a fashion. It includes more than one thousand pictures.

Frans Snyders. 1579–1657. Flanders.
Birds' Concert

Jacob Jordaens (workshop). Flanders.
The Feast of Cleopatra

After Rubens' death, Jacob Jordaens became the leader of the Flemish national
art school. He liked to depict national subjects, as he did in the "Bean King".
"The Feast of Cleopatra" is painted on the known antique subject as
interpreted by the Flemish artist of the mid-17th century. The group of figures
in the foreground filled almost the entire surface of the canvas. The picture is
so overcrowded that hardly can go into its frame. The space is rather
conventional and has no depth, what intensifies an impression of cram and
crash and helps to "reveal" the picture to the viewer. The intensified and
bright colour range underlines a festive impression too.

An idea to depict animals occupied with human
business is not a new one. It is enough to
recollect antique fables, medieval literature and
fairy-tales. Teniers is far from the desire to use
this device in order to create satyrical images or
to affirm some moral ideals. He simply wanted to
depict an amusing scene. The realism in the
representation of monkeys makes the comic
element of the scene even more stronger.

David Teniers the Younger. 1610–1690. Flanders.
Monkeys in the Kitchen

Frans Snyders. 1579–1657. Flanders.
Fruit in a Bowl on a Red Table-Cloth

Frans Hals. Between 1581 and 1585–1666. Holland.
Portrait of a Young Man Holding a Glove. C. 1650

The Tent Room in the New Hermitage

The Tent Room in the New Hermitage was built especially for the pictures of the Minor Dutch school. All genres of painting are represented in this collection. The art of portraiture is presented by two chef-d'oeuvres by Frans Hals, *Portrait of a Man* and *Portrait of a Young Man Holding a Glove*, and by other portraitists. Among numerous landscapes the works of Jacob van Ruisdael stand out. His best work *The Marsh* is a profound philosophical reflection by the artist on nature, life and death.

The "quiet life" of the Dutch still-life is reflected in a multitude of works, one of the masterpieces among them is Willem Heda's *Breakfast with a Lobster* where the objects, bathing in soft silver light, have been placed with a deliberate carelessness on a table. Favourite Dutch genre scenes by Jan Steen, Pieter de Hooch (*A Woman and Her Maid*), Gerard Terborch, Adriaen van Ostade are also found here.

Justus van Huysum. 1659–1716. Holland.
Flowers

Paulus Potter. 1625–1654. Holland.
Dog on a Chain

Pieter de Hooch. 1629–after 1684. Holland.
A Woman and Her Maid. C. 1660

Jan Steen. 1625/26–1679. Holland.
Revellers. C. 1660

Willem Claesz Heda. 1594–between 1680 and 1682. Holland.
Breakfast with Lobster. 1648

Dutch painters managed to combine fidelity to life in depiction of reality and keen feeling for beauty and aesthetic value of an everyday objects how trivial they were. This feature of the Dutch art genius revealed itself best of all in the still life, the most favourite genre in Holland. Dutchmen called it "stilleven" what means "still life". They saw in an inanimate object a kind of hidden life linked with the life of man, his taste, his way of living. Dutch painters used to depict a certain natural disorder in their pictures thus creating an impression of the invisible presence of man in the picture: the pie is cut, the lemon is half-peeled, the wine in the cup is not quite drinken, the candle burns, the book is open and so on. Their still lifes are permeated with a peculiar atmosphere of quieteness and cosyness and give an impression about the measured way of life in the burgher's house where prosperity and peace reign and where every detail says about the host's taste and habbits. The leading still life painters in Holland in the first half of the 17th century were Pieter Claesz and Willem Claesz Heda. Their favourite theme was breakfasts. Objects of quite different forms and texture are put together in the "Breakfast with Lobster": a coffee-pot, glass, lemon, faience dish, silver plate. Willem Heda managed to show the play of light on the surface of glass and metal and created the composition of a refined gray-greenish gamut.

Gerard Terborch. 1617–1681. Holland.
A Glass of Lemonade

Herman van Aldewerelt. 1628/29–1669. Holland.
Musical Party. 1652

Emanuel de Witte. 1616/17–1692. Holland.
Interior View of a Church in Delft

Aert van der Neer. 1603/04–1677. Holland.
A Moonlit Night

Jan Victors. 1619/20–after 1676. Holland.
Ferryboat

Rembrandt Harmensz van Rijn. 1606–1669. Holland.
The Holy Family. 1645

Twenty-four paintings by Rembrandt, one of the best collections in the world, occupy a separate hall. The entire creative path of the great Dutch painter passes before one's eyes with an entire constellation of masterpieces. His early picture *Flora* was painted in the year of the artist's wedding to Saskia van Uylenborch. He depicted his young wife in the sumptuous attire of a goddess with a slightly timid, feminine expression upon a softly illuminated visage. The pride of the collection, created in his mature years, is *Portrait of an Old Man in Red*. Immersed in thought, on the border between light and darkness, life and death, the old man, bearing the yoke of life, is one of the most penetrating and profound images in Rembrandt's art. The protagonist of Rembrandt's most famous painting, *The Return of the Prodigal Son* possesses affinity to it. Painted at the close of the artist's difficult life, rejected in its time, this monumental depiction of an Evangelical scene became the expression of his deep faith in the beauty of human kindness and love.

Rembrandt Harmensz van Rijn. 1606–1669. Holland.
Flora. 1634

Rembrandt Harmensz van Rijn. 1606–1669. Holland.
Danaë. 1636

The fate of Rembrandt's masterpiece, "Danaë", is connected with the Hermitage for more than two centuries. This outstanding canvas was acquird by Catherine II as part of the Crozat collection, and in the autumn of 1772 it was brought to St. Petersburg. By that time the picture's history had more than a century behind. Officially the idea of purchasing the picture was ascribed to Prince Dmitry Golitsyn who was in the 1760s the Russian ambassador to Paris and then, from 1768, to the Hague. The interests of the Russian State in this bargain were represented by Denis Diderot and the Geneva banker and collector of art Françoise Tronchin.
Since the 1870s, when the picture became an object of European scientific researches, interest to it does not fade.
At the early stage, the attention of the researchers was concentrated mainly on the iconographical peculiarities of the work, for the young woman is represented poured not with the rain of gold, but with the bright stream of light.
Danaë is a daughter of Acrisius, the legendary king of Argos, and Euridice (in other sources, Aganippa). Acrisius learnt from the oracle of Delphi that his daughter would give birth to the son who would kill him. In order to avoid the predicted fate, the king ordered to imprison his daughter into a copper cell. However Zeus, struck with Danaë's beauty, poured through the roof in the shape of the gold rain and entered her womb. In the result of this secret unit Danaë gave birth to the son Perseus who mortally wounded his grandfather.
Many a characters of antique myths and history pretended on the role of the heroine of the picture. It is interesting that some researchers considered Danaë to be a personification of purity while others, on the contrary, of vices.
In 1985 an insane man inflicted two knife strikes to the picture and poured onto its surface concentrated sulphuric acid. Thanks to the heroic efforts of the restorers this beautiful painting of the great artist was saved and continues to gladden the visitors to the Hermitage.

Rembrandt Harmensz van Rijn. 1606–1669. Holland.
David's Farewell to Jonathan. 1642

Peter I met in Holland the artist and picture seller Gzell and took him with himself to St. Petersburg to keep his collection of pictures. According to Gzel's words, the tsar liked the pictures of Rubens, Rembrandt, Jan Steen, Wouwerman, Breughel, Ostade and Huysum best of all. The pictures Peter I had brought from Holland were located in the Big Palace and Monplaisir Palace in Peterhof. Later, in 1882, they were transferred to the Hermitage. Through the documents it is known that "David's Farewell to Jonathan" was among the first purchases of masterpieces by West European painters.

Rembrandt Harmensz van Rijn. 1606–1669. Holland.
The Return of the Prodigal Son. C. 1668/69

Rembrandt Harmensz van Rijn. 1606–1669. Holland.
Portrait of an Old Woman. 1654

Rembrandt Harmensz van Rijn. 1606–1669. Holland.
Portrait of an Old Man in Red. C. 1652–54

Claude Gellée (called Lorrain). 1600–1682.
France. Morning in a Harbour. 1640s

The New Hermitage was unable to accommodate the growing collection after 1917. In 1922 the Winter Palace was handed over to the Hermitage by a governmental decree. The exhibition of the French 15th- to 18th-century art, the second most important in the world after the Louvre collection, was displayed in the reserve living quarters with their windows overlooking Palace Square, where Empress Catherine II had resided in the 18th century and which was redecorated in 1837. The works of almost all the French artists are presented here. Twelve pictures acquaint one with the art of Nicolas Poussin, the founder of the French painting school. In one of his best pictures, *Tancred and Erminia*, he ardently and convincingly affirms the beauty of self-sacrifice. Almost all of Antoine Watteau's (1684–1721) eight paintings, which can be considered his masterpieces, are kept here. Watteau was one of a poetic painters of France. Such is his *A Capricious Woman*, a graceful and ironic *scène galante*. Two genre scenes (*The Laundress* and *Grace Before Meal*) and the still-life commissioned by Catherine II represent the serious, pure, humane art of Jean-Baptiste Siméon Chardin.

Simon Vouet. 1590–1649. France.
Allegorical Portrait of Anne of Austria

Ill. on pp. 98–99
Nicolas Poussin. 1594–1665. France.
Tancred and Erminia. 1630s

Ill. on pp. 100–101
Antoine Watteau. 1684–1721. France.
An Embarrassing Proposal. C. 1716

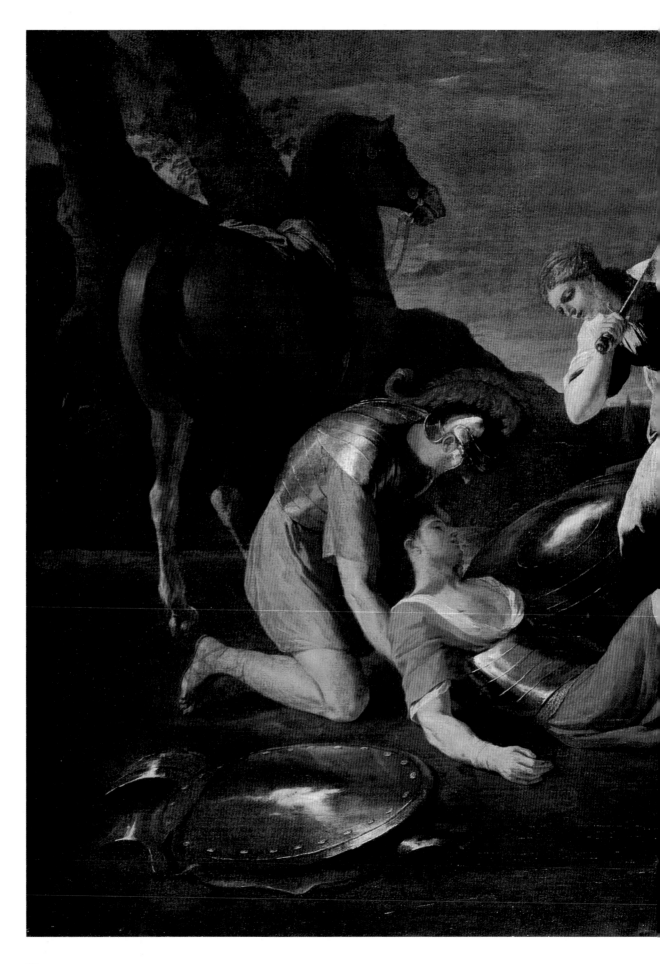

The works of painters hang side by side with outstanding works by leading French sculptors. The jewel of the exhibition is a statue of Voltaire by Jean Antoine Houdon. It is a duplicate of a statue in the foyer of the Comédie-Française in Paris, executed by Houdon on commission of Catherine II.

The collection of the applied arts of France is rich and varied: Limoges enamels and Saint-Porchère faience, the largest in the world collection of 17th- and 18th-century silver, furniture, tapestries, fabrics, embroideries, lace and jewellery. A separate suite of halls was assigned for his collection. The magnificent collection of French graphics, kept in the Departments of Drawing and Engravings, complements this exhibition which in particular comprises one of the best collections of French 16th-century pencil portraiture: the works of François Clouet (*Portrait of Charles IX*) and other masters.

Jean-Baptiste Siméon Chardin. 1699–1779. France.
Grace before Meal. 1744

Ill. on pp. 104–105
Jean-Baptiste Greuze. 1725–1805. France.
A Visit to the Priest. 1786

François Boucher. 1703–1770. France.
Landscape near Beauvais. Early 1740s

François Boucher, Director of the Royal Academy of Painting, a court
painter to Louis XV, author of numerous pictures, drawings and engravings,
was the central figure in the art of the French Rococo which existed,
as contemporaries aptly said, simply "to be pleased with".
He produced stage designs, book illustrations, designs for painted ceilings
and decorative panels, catroons for the Gobelins Manufacture, as well
as models for porcelain articles.
One cannot see images of real people in real background in Boucher's
pictures. His heroes are Venus and Cupids , shepherds and shepherdesses.
Denis Diderot wrote about his pictures: "What a paints! What a diversity...
But where did you see, one asks oneself, shepherds dressed with such
an elegance and splendour?"
The artist prefers an invented beautiful and elegant pastorale to the depiction
of real life. His pictures matched well to the interiors of rooms, for they were
created for French nobility, and the artist kept in mind while painting them
the decorative style of their rooms.

Louis Léopold Boilly. 1761–1845. France.
At the Entrance. 1796–98

Ill. on pp. 108—109
Ferdinand Victor Eugène Delacroix. 1798–1863. France.
Lion Hunt in Morocco. 1854

Eug Delacroix. 1854.

Lucas Cranach the Younger. 1515–1586. Germany.
Christ and Sinner

The exhibition of German 15th- to 18th-century and English 15th- to 19th-century art adjoins the French ones. The works of German Renaissance masters are of special interest, in particular five works by Lucus Cranach the Elder. Painted in 1509, *Venus and Cupid*, is the first depiction of the naked goddess in German art. In accordance with the widespread interpretation of Venus' image in Germany, Cranach imbues his slender goddess with a somewhat menacing countenance. The inscription above her head warns: "Drive away all the temptations of Cupid so that Venus will not take possession of your dazzled heart."

The real name of Lucas Cranach the Elder is, probably, Lucas Maler. Later he chose for his second name the name of his native city of Cranach in Franconia. He began to work in Vienna and then moved to Wittenberg, the main centre of the German Reformation. He was the court painter to the Kurfürst of Saxonia, Frederick III. He joined the Reformation and was a close friend of Martin Luther. Church symbols are present in the picture: the apple-tree is the tree of Eve, a symbol of the original sin expiated by the Virgin Mary, the piece of bread in the Child's hand symbolizes the body of Christ.

Lucas Cranach the Elder. 1472–1553. Germany.
The Madonna and Child under the Apple-Tree

Anton Raphael Mengs. 1728–1779. Germany.
Self-Portrait

Caspar David Friedrich. 1774–1840. Germany.
On the Sailing Boat

John Wootton. C. 1686–1765. England.
Dogs and a Magpie

The exhibits of English art occupies four halls. The pearl of the collection is *Portrait of a Lady in Blue* by Thomas Gainsborough painted masterfully in cold silver-blue tones. Side by side with painting and sculpture, china and faience, one of the best collections of English silver is housed here. A huge silver wine-cooler weighing more than two hundred kilos, standing on figures of lions and decorated with Bacchanal scenes, is executed by Charles Kendler in the first half of the 18th century.

Thomas Gainsborough. 1727–1788. England.
Portrait of a Lady in Blue. Late 1770s

Richard Brompton. 1734–1783. England.
Portrait of Great Dukes Alexander and Constantine

Joshua Reynolds. 1723–1792. England.
Cupid Untying the Zone of Venus. 1788

The exhibition of Contemporary Art of the 19th–20th centuries is located on the second floor. The largest collection of French Impressionism, Post-Impressionnism and early 20th-century masters is housed here. These paintings were collected at the border of the 19th and 20th centuries by Moscow collectors, Sergei Shchukin and the Morozov brothers, Ivan and Mikhail. Nationalized after the 1917 revolution, they constituted the Museum of Contemporary Western Art in Moscow. After its closure in 1948 the collections were divided between the Pushkin Museum of Fine Art in Moscow and the Hermitage. The heroic struggle of French painters for a new, contemporary art, is reflected in the Hermitage in works by leading artists. Eight pictures by Claude Monet reveal the formation of the Impressionist method. The companion pictures, *Corner of the Garden at Montgerons* and *Pond in Mongerons*, created in 1876, marked the blossoming of Impressionism: from scattered fine coloured dabs, hurled onto the canvas, a lively and palpitating world of nature is born, infused with sunlight and fanned by the wind. The most renowned of six pictures by Auguste Renoir is *Portrait*

Claude Oscar Monet. 1840–1926. France.
Lady in the Garden (Sainte-Adresse). 1867

The summer of 1867 Oscar Monet spent, at the request of his father, in Sainte-Adresse, in the house of his aunt. He wrote to Bazile in his letter of June 25: "I have more than enough things to be done, twenty canvases are started already, the astonishing marines, and figures, and gardens, and many things else." He achieved an impressive treatment of sunlight in his landscapes painted in Sainte-Adresse. It is known that the woman in the picture is the wife of his cousin, Jeanne Margueritte Lecadre, but Monet did not want to make a portrait. He was attracted by a complicated task of depicting the woman's white dress lit by the sun. That is why he later painted over the figure of a man that initially was at the right side of the lady.

Pierre Auguste Renoir. 1841–1919. France.
Girl with a Fan. 1881

Paul Cézanne. 1839–1906. France.
Big Pine-Tree near Aix. 1890s

of the Actress Jeanne Samary. The play of light and colour is evoked by a charming femininity and the elusive delicate mood of the young actress, depicted in the foyer of the theatre.

Eleven pictures by Cézanne—landscapes, portraits and still-lifes—reveal the talent of the great Post-Impressionist master to the fullest. His *Big Pine-Tree near Aix*, represents a tree warmed by the sun, inserting its hand-like branches in the goldish distances and blue sky of Provence, and is an embodiment of living energy and strength. Dutch by nationality, Van Gogh became a great French artist. *Ladies of Arles*, created, as his other three pictures, at the zenith of his talent, in Provence in 1888, hang next to the peasant woman of his Dutch drawings. A single violently flourishing earth cultivated by human hands united them. All twenty-five of Paul Gauguin's pictures were painted in Oceania, where he set off, realizing his dream about "a piece of earth untouched by civilization". His *Tahitian Pastorales* is an embodiment in colour

of an acquired faith of the artist in the harmony of the universe. The sculptures of Auguste Rodin are assigned an entire hall. Like his contemporary Impressionists he strove to imbue life with movement (*Eternal Spring*), subordinating it to marble and bronze.

The extensive division of the exhibition acquaints one with the early art of the best 20th-century masters. The famous French painter Henri Matisse once said: "My best works are in the Leningrad". One of his twenty-seven works is *Red Room*. Its protagonist, red colour, subordinates all the hues to itself. Colour harmony here is not the virtue of a beautiful interior but the sign of beauty, not formal but infused with the warmth of human existence. Some thirty works by Pablo Picasso represents the Red, Blue and Cubist periods of his art. *Lady with a Fan* is one of the most famous works of Cubism. The picture contains an allusion to the theme (its second title is *After the Ball*), but it does not contain a narrative: the objective construction of the female image is naked. The

Henri Matisse. 1869–1954. France.
Vase of Irises. 1912

Paul Gauguin. 1843–1903. France.
Woman Holding a Fruit. 1893

Paul Signac. 1863–1935. France.
Harbour in Marseilles

great sound of a mighty symphony in the *Composition No. 6* by the founder of Abstractionism, Wassily Kandinsky, completes the exhibition of art from the nineteenth-early twentieth centuries. Adjoining it is the hall dedicated to contemporary Iitalian art. Geometrically strict forms and the pure colour of the *Metaphysical Still-Life* by Georges Morandi reveals the talent of one of the founders of the "metaphysical painting". A vast section comprises the works of outstanding 20th-century sculptors.

Paul Signac was a follower of Georges Seurat who invented a new painting device called divisionism. It was developed on the base of Post-Impressionism. According to this method the surface of the picture is to be covered with separate small dubs of pure colour. While being seen from a distance, they mix optically but not on the artist's palette, as it was in practice before. Seurat's technique is often called Pointillism. Many critics believed that the new method diminished the individuality of the artist converting his creative process into a rather dull and pedantic work.

Kees van Dongen. 1877–1968. France.
Red Dancer. C. 1907

Ill. on pp. 128–129
Wassily Kandinsky. 1866–1944. Germany.
Composition No. 6

Bartolommeo Carlo Rastrelli. 1675–1744. Russia.
Bust portrait of Peter I

The exhibits from the Department of the History of Russian Culture of the 6th-early 20th centuries is located on the first floor of the palace—relics of the applied arts and mode of life, technology and sciences, paintings and sculptural portraits, drawings and engravings. The Sections of Slavonic and Old Russian Culture are side by side with the objects of crafts, ancient Russian frescoes and around one thousand icons, which includes a not inconsiderable number of veritable masterpieces. Numerous exhibits tell about Peter I's era (the first quarter of the 18th century) including personal and memorial things belonging to Peter himself. One of the halls is designed like an interior of a wealthy house of that period. A table with folded painted leafs, executed for Peter by craftsmen from Arkhangelsk, is in the centre; and one of the first Russian tapestries depicting Peter I at the Battle of Poltava hangs on the wall. A bronze bust of Peter I is an outstanding work of the Italian sculptor Bartholommeo Carlo Rastrelli (the father of the architect), invited to Russia by Peter and working here all his life.

Among pieces of furniture, costumes, china, silver, carved bone, Tula steel and others, which present the "century of Empresses" (the reign of Elizabeth Petrovna and Catherine II)

Winter Palace of Peter I

While restoring the Hermitage Theatre the parts of the Winter Palace of Peter I were discovered. Later a special exposition devoted to the great reformer was organized there. The interior of the early 18th century was re-created, and the "wax person" of Peter I made of wood and wax by Bartolommeo Carlo Rastrelli was transferred there. The Hermitage has a unique collection of lathes from the tsar's turneries which were located in the Peter's palace and in the Summer Gardens. Of the eleven lathes that have come to our time, the most known is one, which has the first in Russia support. It was made by the well-known inventors, A. Nartov and F. Singer in 1718-29. The enthusiasm for turning was widely spread at the German princely courts in the 17th-18th centuries. It is known that Maximilian I was among its enthusiasts whose lathe has come up to our time. The Copenhagen Kunstkammer boasts with articles turned by Emperor Rudolf II and Frederick V of Denmark.

Ivan Vishniakov. 1688–1761. Russia.
Portrait of Stepanida Yakovleva. C. 1756

Boudoir in the Rococo style. Russia. 19th century

with pageantry, the portraits, often created by the best 18th-century painters, are of especial interest. One of them, Ivan Vishniakov's portrait of Stepanida Yakovleva, the fiance of the son of a Petersburg merchant, unites in itself the devices of the European portrait with elements of the ancient Russian *parsuna*. The private chambers of Nicholas I's family are occupied by the exhibition "Russian Nineteenth-Century Interiors", combining furniture, tapestries, china and portraiture. These are items from the Winter Palace and other tsar's residences and private palaces and mansions of St. Petersburg.

The ground floor of the Winter Palace is under the disposal of the Archaeological Department. Its exhibitions include objects of Primitive Culture from the Paleolithic era to the first centuries of our millennium, discovered by archaeologists (or accidentally) on the territory of Russia, Ukraine or the Black Sea Coast. One of the halls contains the finds from the burial-mound of a leader from the 5th–4th centuries B.C., unearthed between 1929 and 1954 in a barrow in the Pazyryk settlement in the Altai. The permafrost formed in the grave preserved unique objects of ancient art: a huge felt carpet of local workmanship, a wooden funeral chariot, ornaments in the Animal Style of wood, leather, felt, Chinese silk and also the oldest in the world wool pile Persian (or Middle Asian) carpet. The culture of the Scythian nomad tribes dwelling in the steppes of the Black Sea coast between the 7th and the 3rd centuries B.C. is presented in an extensive exhibition of objects from Scythian burial-mounds and settlements. The famous collection of Scythian gold is kept in a special storeroom. The gold pendant in the form of a deer from the late 7th century B.C.–6th century B.C. is a masterpiece of the Scythian Animal Style. It was discovered in 1897 near Kostromskaya settlement in the Northern Caucasus. The

Shield decoration. 7th–6th centuries B.C.
From the excavations of the Kostromskaya
Barrow

The famous Scythian gold plates once decorating
the chiefs' shields, originate from the burial
mound of the 6th century B.C. and were studied
in Kuban. The panther was discovered in one of
the barrows near the Kelermess station in 1903.
The deer was found in the barrow near the
village of Kostromskaya in 1897. For the
Scythian art the so-called "Animal Style" is
characteristic. It is characterized with depictions
of animals fighting or tormenting their prey.
Notwithstanding the conventionality and
summary character of the forms, the craftsmen
managed to skillfully and quite naturally depict
the alertly raised head of the deer or the smooth
movement of the panther. The deer for Scythians
was the symbol of the sun.

deer decorating the shield of a Scythian warrior was considered a solar symbol, signifying the positive forces of nature. The outer appearance of the Scythians, their character are magnificently evoked in their depiction decorating the gold comb of the 4th-century B.C. from the Solokha barrow unearthed in 1912–13 on the bank of the Dnieper. This is a masterpiece from the Bosporus kingdom, established by the Greeks in the Crimea in the 6th century B.C.

The Oriental Department boasts more than 150,000 objects of art and culture of the peoples of the East. The art of the ancient Orient—Egypt and Mesopotamia—is exhibited on the ground floor of the Winter Palace. The relatively small collections reflect all the historical stages of Ancient Egyptian art. The collection of sculptures—statues, portraits, reliefs from palaces and tombs, bronze and clay statuettes—as well as painted sarcophagi, papyri and Faym portraits, relating to the later period of the 1st–3rd centuries A.D., and Coptic cloths from Christian Egypt (4th–9th centuries) are of great interest.

The exhibition devoted to the art of Central Asian countries is on the ground floor also. Among the manifold exhibits—items of ceramic and metal, carpets, weapons and others—the enormous frescoes with depictions of hunting scenes and

festivals, which once decorated in the 5th–7th centuries the walls of the palaces of dignitaries excavated in the ancient town of Pendjkent, occupy a special place.

The exhibition of Byzantine art (4th–15th centuries) occupies three halls on the second floor of the Winter Palace. It is a marvellous collection of silver ecclesiastical vessels, enamels, articles of carved bone nd icons. The best icon in the collection, the icon of St. Gregory the Thaumaturgist (12th century), is distinguished by a delicateness of brushwork, wealth of colours and an especial intellectuality of the image. A large exhibition of art of Near Eastern countries is housed in the neighbouring halls. The exhibits of Iranian art contain one of the best collections in the world of silver articles from the Sassanid dynasty era (3rd–7th centuries). Among their masterpieces is a dish with a depiction of Emperor Shapur II (309–379) hunting. The second floor also houses a rich exhibit from Far Eastern countries—China, Tibet, Mongolia, India, Indonesia and Japan. The Chinese articles embrace the period from the 13th century B.C. to the beginning of the 20th century, these are china, enamel, carved stones, and lacquerware adjoining paintings and items of plastic arts.

Unique objects were collected by Russian scholars during excavations. Murals, painted loess statuettes and two clay figures of fantastic beasts—Guardians of Buddha's Throne— were delivered in 1914–15 from Turkestan from the Cave Monastery of the Thousand Buddhas in Dun Xuang (4th century). The collection of paintings includes both a marvellous collection of Buddhist icons and 11th- to 15th-century secular paintings on silk, as well as works of contemporary painters.

The exposition of Chinese art
in the Winter Palace. 18th–20th centuries

A folding screen made of Koromandel lacquer
is on the display in this room. The name of the
lacquer came from the Bay of Koromandel on
the eastern shore of India through which these
articles found their way to Europe. The screen
is made in the first half of the 18th century of
wood covered, over the gesso ground, with black
lacquer and decorated, on the one side, with
coloured depiction of scenes of court life and
the flowers-and-birds motifs, on the other side.

Vases of chalcedone and nephrite. China.
18th century

Besides wonderful pieces of China porcelain,
lacquer, cloisonnée and painted enamels great
place in the collection is occupied by articles
of carved stones—more than one hundred items.
Made of nephrite, rock crystal, chalcedone,
topaz, amethyst and other stones, these things impress
one not only by the diversity of motifs and forms,
but by the skill in the understanding of the
texture of the material and the ability of the
master to subordinate this hard material to the
master's will.

The Hermitage Theatre is an inseparable part of the Hermitage. It was built in 1783–87 by the architect Giacomo Quarenghi by the order of Catherine II. The theatre is connected with the Old Hermitage by the gallery on the arch over the Winter Canal where the theatre foyer is housed. Catherine II organized suppers in it after performances which generally consummated the Hermitage reception. In 1902 Leonty Benois designed the foyer in the style of French eighteenth-century Rococo. From the foyer one can enter the authentic 18th-century theatre hall. It was built in the form of an ancient amphitheatre: six rows of benches descend onto a small pit in front of the stage—armchairs were placed here for the Empress. In our day performances are staged in the theatre and public lectures are read. The hall and stage were built by Quarenghi in the Winter Palace of Peter I which was located at this site so that its socle part was preserved. Almost 200 years later, in 1987–89, during the restoration of the theatre the private chambers of Peter I, which had been located here, were reconstructed and opened for visitors. The "wax person" of the emperor was placed in his study—a depiction of Peter I in his natural size of wood and wax, executed by Carlo Bartholommeo Rastrelli. The "person" is arrayed in the formal dress of Peter I with a ribbon and star of the order of St. Andrew the First-Called.

The spirit of the Petrine epoch is revived in the chambers of the Menshikov Palace, one of the first palaces of St. Petersburg, which was built in the 1710s–1720s for the first Petersburg Governor-General, the closet associate of Peter I, Alexander Menshikov. The recreated part of the private chambers, official and servant quarters, as a result of the restoration in the 1950–1970s, provides an idea about the life of their brilliant proprietor–one of the most striking personalities of the Petrine era.

From the formal antechamber decorated with antique sculptures, which alongside with othert works of art Menshikov collected following an example of his great patron, Peter I, the oak stairway leads to the first floor, where the Great Hall was located. Light, with gilt ornamentations and mirrors, the hall was used for receptions and "assemblies" at which Peter gathered all the nobilities of the new capital by his order. The living quarters of the owner were also on the first floor. In the suite of living rooms., the Walnut Study lavishly decorated with a panel of different kinds of precious wood, placed between the pilastres with carved gilded capitals, is especially alluring.

The Hermitage Theatre

The State Hermitage is not only a world famous museum. It comprises a unique realm, a special page of Russian history. The founder of St. Petersburg, Peter I, died here, Catherine the Great directed affairs of state and Nicholas II inaugurated the first State Duma. These walls recall Alexander I, the victor over Napoleon, the Tsar-Liberator Alexander II, who died from wounds, and the arrest of the Provisional Government by revolutionary soldiers and sailors in 1917. These walls also recall the terrible days of the Great Patriotic War when museum workers, who were dying of hunger, salvaged monuments of art for posterity. In creating its interiors, the architects, sculptors, artists and decorators, who conceived this magnificent ensemble, realized their ideas about the beautiful; they carried the spirit of an era long passed down to us and established that special inner world which underscores the value of works of art and allows one on every occasion to apprehend their significance. The curators and keepers of the Hermitage collections, as well as all other members of the stuff, do their best in keeping the traditions of their predecessors trying not only to preserve the great heritage of the past but to develop the museum according to new trends. At the same time nobody forgets that the Hermitage is not only a world-famous museum, but an evidence of Russian history which must be dear to every Russian.

The Winter Palace viewed from Palace Square

GROUND FLOOR

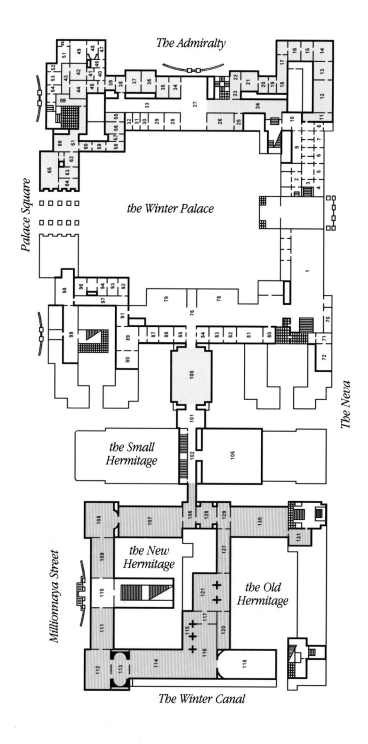

The Admiralty

The Neva

The Winter Palace

the Winter Palace

Palace Square

the Small Hermitage

the New Hermitage

the Old Hermitage

Millionnaya Street

The Winter Canal

Oriental Art and Culture

34–39. Art and Culture of Central Asia
(4th century B.C.–12th century A.D.)

55–65. Art and Culture of the Caucasus
(10th century B.C.–16th century A.D.)

66–69. Art and Culture of Golden Horde
(13th–14th centuries)

41–45. The Special Vault of the East
Department

100. Art and Culture of Ancient Egypt
(4th millenium B.C.–6th century A.D.)

*Art and Culture of Classical
Antiquity*

111–114, 121. Art and Culture of Ancient
Greece (7th–2nd centuries B.C.)

115–117. Art and Culture of Ancient Towns in
the Northern Black Sea Coast Region
(8th century B.C.–3rd century A.D.)

130–131. Art and Culture of Ancient Italy
(7th–2nd centuries B.C.)

106–109, 127–129. Art of Ancient Rome
(1st century B.C.–early 4th century A.D.)

Primitive Art and Culture

11. Culture of the Palaeolithic and Mesolithic
Ages (300,000–7000 B.C.)

12–14, 24. Culture of the Neolithic, Bronze
and Iron Ages (5000–500 B.C.)

15–18. Art and Culture of the Scythians
(8th–3rd centuries B.C.)

19, 20. Population of Forest-steppes
(7th–4th centuries B.C.)

21–23, 26. Objects excavated in the Altai
mounds

26. Objects excavated in the Pazyryk mounds

33. Art and Culture of the Southern Steppes of
the Former USSR (3rd century B.C.–10th
century A.D.)

24. Art and Culture of the Forest and Forest-
steppe Regions in Eastern Europe
(7th century B.C.–12th century A.D.)

FIRST FLOOR

Western European Art

259. Western European Applied Art: 11th–15th centuries

207–224, 229–238. Italian Art: 13th–18th centuries

239, 240. Spanish Art: 15th–19th centuries

248, 258, 261–262. Netherlandish Art: 15th–early 17th centuries

245–247. Flemish Art: 17century

249–252, 254. Dutch Art: 17 century

263–268. German Art: 15th–18 centuries

272–281, 283–297. French Art: 15th–18th centuries

298–302. English Art: 17th–19th centuries

243. Western European Arms and Armour: 15th–17th centuries

195. Western European Silver: 17th–18th centuries

269–271. Western European Porcelain: 18th century

200, 201, 303. Western European Tapestries

241. Gallery of Old Painting

Russian Culture

147–150. Russian Culture: 10th–15th centuries

151–152. Culture of the Muscovite Russia: 15th–17th centuries

153, 155–161. Russian Culture: late 17th–first quarter of the 18th century

162–173. Russian Culture: 1750–1800

175–187. Russian Interiors: 19th century

189. The Malachite Room: exhibition of malachite objects produced by Russian craftsmen in the first half of the 19th century

197. The 1812 Gallery

190–195, 198. Halls of the temporary exhibitions

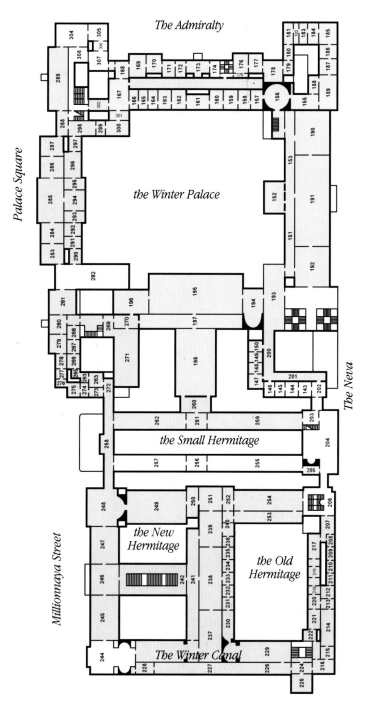

The Admiralty

Palace Square

the Winter Palace

The Neva

Millionnaya Street

the Small Hermitage

the New Hermitage

the Old Hermitage

The Winter Canal

SECOND FLOOR

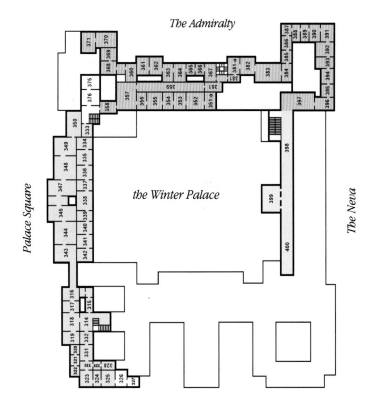

The Admiralty

the Winter Palace

Palace Square

The Neva